THE MOON AND STARS OF THE DARK NIGHT SKY

POEMS OF CELESTE AND HER SOPHIA

BETHANY DAVIS

Caer Illandria Enterprises
P.O. Box 7557, Broomfield, CO 80021
www.caerillandria.com

ISBN: 0692430717
ISBN-13: 978-0692430712

For my Sophia, my muse, my song, my love. It is for you my heart sings and for you poetry comes to life.

CONTENTS

The morning wind spreads its fresh smell. We must get up and take that in, that wind that lets us live. Breathe before it's gone.

— Jalāl ad-Dīn Muhammad Rūmī

Bethany Davis

The Night Devours You

Inspired by the words of an amazing girl,

including some of hers

Look to the sky,
Feel the Night's presence.
Night's embrace,
The arms of Darkness hold you.
The Night envelops you,
It is hungry,
The Night devours you.
Lost in it.

As you are consumed,
You consume.
As the night devours you,
You devour.
Consumed becomes consumer,
Devouring yourself, one with yourself.
The Night and you are one.

Standing in the Void of Space,
Alone,
But not alone.
You are Night,
You are God Herself,
Nuit, full of stars.
Complete in yourself,
Unneeding,
Eternally satisfied.

The Mirror before you,
Yourself, looking at yourself,
In the Dark Mirror,
The curve of space.
Complete and alone,
Not alone.
Other.
Self.

You step towards.
She steps towards.
Night sees Night,
Embrace,
Passion.
She is you.
You are Night.
She is Night.
One.

Love, ecstasy.
Coupling, self with self.
Sex.
Orgasm.
Power.
Consumed.
Lost.

Bethany Davis

Worlds spin away,
Creation begins.
Light out of Darkness.
Let there be light.
Shaking from passion.
Vibrations between atoms.
Night, proton.
Electron and neutron,
Twins, Divine Twins.
Big Bang, Big Orgasm.
Stars, the substance of stars.
Every man and woman is a star.

When it is dark enough, you can see the stars.

~April 19, 2011

Bethany Davis

Bethany Davis

Sophia Stood in Darkness

"I was formed long ages ago,
at the very beginning, when the world came to be.
When there were no watery depths, I was given birth,
when there were no springs overflowing with water;
before the mountains were settled in place,
before the hills, I was given birth"
Proverbs 8:23-25

Sophia stood in darkness,
Her voice rang out to me.
I walked with her in darkness,
Her arm was around me.

She placed her feet before us,
Each step brought light to me.
Creation formed behind us,
With each step the world was made.

Her tears flowed down around me,
They washed me in their light.
Her sorrow raw before me,
I want to dry them with a kiss.

Her beauty ever flowing,
From deep within her breast.
She cannot see that beauty,
But it's there for all to see.

We stop when we have made it,
We turn to see what came before.
Creation stretches behind us,
For in the journey, the world is made.

~April 28, 2011

Bethany Davis

I Turn

Celeste, Selene, Luna.
Moonlight on water, wind across the waves,
Night's sweet embrace.
I rise from the water,
Dripping, flowing, down my naked back.
Cold wind, I shiver, exposed but free.
Moonlight on water drops, my skin pale.
Peaceful night, silent, alone.
Not alone.
Eyes on me.
I turn.

~May 2, 2011

Bethany Davis

Bethany Davis

An Eternal Knot

What's distance to a soul?
What's time, what's space?
A thousand life times, a thousand miles,
  A second, an inch.
    Two souls connected,
      Never separated,
        Reaching through time,
          Reaching through space.
A touch, a brush, a whisper,
  A thin thread,
    Shorter than an atom,
      Longer than all time.
Two souls,
  Knitted together,
    An eternal knot.

~May 2, 2011

Bethany Davis

There She Stands

A room, faded, indistinct,
A room of dreams,
The edges blurred,
Distant,
Unnecessary,
Out there is lost,
Unknown,
Not important,
Forgotten,
Only the present,
Only here,
Nothing else.

There she stands,
By herself,
Isolated,
Alone,
Sadness,
Pain,
Feeling like there's nothing.

There she stands,
In the middle of the room,
The floor strone with tea cups,
Broken,
Smashed,
Like her dreams,
Like her memories,
Spread across the floor,
Jagged,
Sharp,
Like the pain she knows.

There she stands,
On the shards,
On the tea cups,
The symbol of polite society,
Of normality,
Of privilege,
Of a life lived properly,
The fear of the cage it brings,
To live another's dream,
To be what they say,
To act how they act,
To not know herself,
To not know freedom,
The dance of ecstasy,
In the rain at night,
Under moonlight,
Untamed,
Wild,
Free.

There she stands,
On the shards,
On the tea cups,
Sharp,
Jagged,
Cutting,
Tearing,
Her feet in sheds,
The skin,
The meat,
Hanging,
Like the meat of a butchered deer,
Torn from bone,
Torn,
By the shards of her broken life.

Bethany Davis

The shards,
Spread across the floor,
Covered in her blood,
Her essence,
Poured out on the floor,

Dripping,
Flowing,
Bright red against white ceramics,
Baptising the shards of her broken life.

Torn feet,
Full of pain,
Pain of the body,
Pain of the soul,
Of her loneliness,
Of her doubts,
Her forgotten dreams,
Dashed to the floor like tea cups,
Shattering before her eyes.

The pain stirs her,
She stirs,
Moves,
Awakes,
From the dreams of pain,
Healing comes,
From her blood,
Bloody tea cups,
Her freedom comes,
Awakens,
Arises,
Reborn.

~May 17, 2011

Bethany Davis

Bethany Davis

Night's Wind

The dark surrounds,
Enfolds,
Fills all,
Hides all,
Secrets and mysteries,
Danger and terror,
Peace and calm.
The wind blows,
Out of the night,
Out of the darkness,
Moving hair,
Moving leaves and grass,
Pushing,
Pulling,
Something alive,
Something strong,

Like a hand,
Grabbing,
Taking,
Trying to take.
Is the wind the darkness?
Is the darkness the wind?
Dark wind,
Night's wind,
Fair Nyx lost in shadow,
Reaching out,
Grabbing,
Taking,
Trying to take,
A wind on skin and hair,
A darkness that can be felt,
Hungry,
Consuming,
Dark wind,
Night's wind.

~October 8, 2011

Bethany Davis

Wisdom of the Moon

It's said that back in days of old,
The nights were lit by Celeste's light,
Pale white light in darkest night,
Moon and stars that light the night.

The lesser mystery of her shining light,
Many seek but so few do find,
Shining bright the Goddess White,
Moon and stars that light the night.

But deeper still and hard to find,
The greater mystery Sophia's light,
Hidden light in darkest night,
The night itself the Goddess Black.

Wisdom's shadow, Sophia's light,
Pitch black dark but lit by stars,
The night is darkest before the dawn,
The wisdom's spark hidden deep within.

Celeste's light is clear to see,
The moon, the stars, that light the night,
But Sophia's light is hard to find,
Few part the veil to find its source.

~May 27, 2012

Bethany Davis

For Whom Do I Wait

For whom do I wait for and for whom do I long,
Through ages and times long past?
Whose touch is it that shakes my soul,
With joy and pleasure full?
Across my back a gentle touch,
That tickles as much as thrills.
Along me sides, I rise to meet,
And kisses my naked neck.
Astride my waist, my shoulders rub,
A weight that comforts and warms.
Along my arms, a gentle stroke,
That raises bumps across my skin.
Moving down on my feet to sit,
And rubs my upraised rear.
And down my thighs and my calves,
And my feet never knew such joy.
You roll me over, my front exposed,
Your smile that makes me blush.
Up my legs your hands to roam,
And outward up my hips.
Once more you sit across my waist,
And now our eyes do meet.
Leaning down, you kiss my lips,
And from them comes a sign.
You kiss my cheeks and then my nose,
And then my waiting neck.
My eyes are closed as your hands they roam,
And move across my breasts.
I purr, I stretch, I love your touch,
The play of fingers deft.

How is your touch so well known,
Why do I know it so?

For whom do I wait for and for whom do I long,
Through ages and times long past?
Whose touch is it that shakes my soul,
With joy and pleasure full?
Your kisses come, first on my neck,
And then you kiss my chest.
Down between my lovely breast,
Your kisses pull my heart.
Round the bottom up the sides,
Your lips upon my breast.
Soft as snow and warm as fire,
And wet like springtime dew.
My flesh it moves, alive and free,
Delighting in your kiss.
Flesh to flesh, lip to breast,
Ecstatic joyous me.
First one breast and then the other,
Consuming all of me.
I quiver there beneath your hips,
And beneath your steamy breath.
I'm drowning here in ecstatic joy,
Beneath your loving kiss.
A way to die I'd be glad to have,
An ocean of your love.
Then you stop and give me breath,
And let me settle down.
You look at me with loving eyes,
In them I am lost.
A smile you give, a crooked smile,
That bodes I know not what.
You hands them move, they touch my breasts,
Then settle at my waist.

Bethany Davis

You moved down, I know not when,
For I was lost in bliss.
My waist held firm, your hips descend,
Now I'm like a bed.
Your searching kiss my belly finds,
It tickles and delights.
In circles slow with movements fair,
I giggle on my back.
And down you go, you kiss my hips,
One kiss on either side.
You kiss my mound, you move on down,
Your lips that do delight.
Once more I think and wonder why,
I swear I know your touch.

For whom do I wait for and for whom do I long,
Through ages and times long past?
Whose touch is it that shakes my soul,
With joy and pleasure full?
Your lips are soft, your gentle kiss,
Wet and fully there.
Kiss of delights that finds me there,
Kiss at my most hidden place.
A moving tongue, a searching kiss,
A building wave within.
Forever lost in sweet embrace,
A flower in the spring.
Petals part and nectar flows,
Consumed with daring care.
A flower opened for your joy,
And pleasure for myself.

~June 1, 2014

Bethany Davis

Flutters

Butterflies flutter
  in a cage of flesh,
A gentle discomfort
  that speaks of joy,
Wonder they do
  of what might come,
But happy and nervous
  and waiting for it,
A blush or a flush
  a longing and want,
All things are possible
  the butterflies say,
What needed risks
  will be made sure,
When those wings
  are open,
When those wings
  are free?

~January 7, 2015

Bethany Davis

Deep Within

There's an ache in my heart each time we part,
And a flutter each time we talk,
And the joy you bring is like not one thing,
I have ever felt before,
And in your eyes I find delight,
My own reflected back,
And the feeling grows deep within,
That you bring forth from me to grow.

My Sophia dear you're my heart's delight,
And all I want to know,
My day and night like the sun so bright,
In your shadowed small abode,
I long for you with all my soul,
And pine when we're apart,
And the feeling grows deep within,
That you bring forth from me to grow.

The years have past and so much has changed,
But still you're all my heart,
And the past bars and cupboard doors,
Have all long passed away,
Shadows dance with the fire so bright,
And shines within your eyes,
And the feeling grows deep within,
That you bring forth from me to grow.

Each moment past that we have talked,
Has been a balm upon my soul,
And each fine word in jest or love,
Has woken me all the more,
I want your touch and to feel your lips,
And to be right by your side,
And the feeling grows deep within,
That you bring forth from me to grow.

There's an ache in my heart each time we part,
And a flutter each time we talk,
And the joy you bring is like not one thing,
I have ever felt before,
And in your eyes I find delight,
My own reflected back,
And the feeling grows deep within,
That you bring forth from me to grow.

~January 13, 2015

Bethany Davis

Shattered

It's my scars I bared,
To her last night,
Like all the hounds of Hel,
My shattered, broken, war scarred soul,
Laid raw to the winter air,
A thousand tea cups shattered there,
Lie broken on the floor,
Like knives that cut and blades that slice,
The rawness of the soul,
From cupboard doors thrown open wide,
They tumbled to the ground,
And bloody footprint across the floor,
Where she walked away for now.

~January 18, 2015

Bethany Davis

Bethany Davis

Twining Hearts

Twining hearts and twining lives,
Two lives intertwined,
I'm drawn to her through all the years,
I knew her all my life,
She speaks to me with words that hear,
That know my every move,
She sees me true through all the years,
She sees me all complete,
A dance we dance through all the years,
A dance that ever moves,
In the stillness and in the peace,
Changing all the time,
Like two trees grown side by side,
That twist around and round,
They grow as one and grow entwined,
Until they are one tree,
And through the years and through all time,
There is no other way,
Two hearts entwined must find their match,
In each others' eyes,
Twining hearts and twining lives,
Two lives intertwined,
I'm drawn to her through all the years,
I knew her all my life.

~February 5, 2015

Bethany Davis

Bethany Davis

Whisper in the Night

With a wistful whisper,
She said good night,
A linger in my mind.

And one word rang out,
Through the air,
That whisper in the night.

Bye she said,
In a wistful tone,
Reluctance to let go.

And one word rang out,
Through the air,
That whisper in the night.

The sound it was,
Like music's ring,
An echo through my mind.

And one word rang out,
Through the air,
That whisper in the night.

Just like a kiss,
It came to me,
And touched my very soul.

And one word rang out,
Through the air,
That whisper in the night.

Bethany Davis

Lingering kiss,
My very soul,
Reluctant for lips to part.

And one word rang out,
Through the air,
That whisper in the night.

That last raw kiss,
Of love and lose,
A whisper on my lips.

And one word rang out,
Through the air,
That whisper in the night.

For love is loss,
And loss is love,
The parted will then return.

And one word rang out,
Through the air,
That whisper in the night.

Bye she said,
In a wistful tone,
Reluctance to let go.

And one word rang out,
Through the air,
That whisper in the night.

And one word rang out,
Through the air,
That whisper in the night.

~February 9, 2015

All

Across the stars of a million years,
And all that's come and gone,
I walk with you, my heart, my soul,
And all I long to be.

You are my hopes, you are my dreams,
My lover through eternity,
I walk with you, my heart, my soul,
And all I hope to be.

If we're together or we're apart,
You're always here with me,
I walk with you, my heart, my soul,
And all I want to be.

The stars and moon in the midnight sky,
Me in your loving arms,
I walk with you, my heart, my soul,
And all I need to be.

~February 13, 2015

Bethany Davis

Bethany Davis

Only Love

Longing I feel in my very soul,
For my only love,
The distance that stands in the way,
Is hard, so hard to bear,
But in my heart and in my soul,
You're ever here with me,
And the distance is but for a time,
And in your arms I'll be,
I miss you love, my only love,
I long for your embrace,
And in your arms I will soon rest,
The waiting finally done,
You are my soul, you are my heart,
My one and only love,
My tomcat, sexy wildcat,
My only delight,
And so I wait for that day to come,
When I do come to you,
And in your arms I will soon rest,
The waiting finally done.

~February 15, 2015

Bethany Davis

Fading to Black

There we stand in the setting sun,
Beauty all around,
Into your eyes I look and gaze,
As you look back at me,
We're silhouettes against the light,
No details for all to see,
But in your eyes I see all time,
And see both you and I,
The light may shine and the light may fade,
But you my only one,
Are ever there if near or far,
Ever in my soul,
Your gentle hands and strong strong hold,
Like you're afraid to let go,
I smile there as your eyes enfold,
For you are the world to me,
And as the last of the evening light,
Fades from orange to blue to grey,
I know deep done the sun will rise,
And start another day,
For though we part we always return,
And goodbye is never done,
In your eyes I'll look again,
As I have always done,
So in the dark with the light long gone,
And us both but dark dark shapes,
You hold my hands and still we gaze,
And all else fades to black.

~February 18, 2015

Bethany Davis

Pain of Sorrow

Pain of sorrow,
Pain of guilt,
Year by year,
It will not quit,
It does not fade,
But ever grows,
Pain of sorrow,
Pain of guilt.

Pain of sorrow,
Pain of guilt,
What could have been,
What did not come,
Blaming self,
For pain or death,
Pain of sorrow,
Pain of guilt.

Arise my love,
And spread your wings,
Like your life,
Not one gone,
Open your eyes,
And see the moon,
Arise my love,
And spread your wings.

Arise my love,
And spread your wings,
Let memories,
Forever live,
But let the guilt,
Now fade away,
Arise my love,
And spread your wings.

~February 21, 2015

Spinning

I dance a dance through eternity,
  with you there by my side,
Around we go and all things change,
  and yet they stay the same,
You are my love, my lover dark,
  the night sky spinning round,
And round we go and all things change,
  and yet they stay the same,
Though we part at times, we do return,
  in this eternal dance,
Each moment apart it breaks my heart,
  but oh I love return,
I dance a dance through eternity,
  with you there by my side,
Around we go and all things change,
  and yet they stay the same,
You are my love, my lover dark,
  the night sky spinning round.

~March 6, 2015

Bethany Davis

Bethany Davis

My Flight to You

Up I go into the sky,
To go to my true love,
Under clouds and through the mist,
That obscures what's far below.

Fear and worry plague my mind,
But hope is everlasting,
What is what is, what comes must come,
And joy will greet me there.

Why do I fear, why do I fret,
When love is where I go,
Over rock and over snow,
Gliding through the sky.

And whispered thoughts, lost memories,
All do speak of her,
What parts must part, but comes again,
Why worry when I crave?

Bethany Davis

And round and round the worries go,
Through thought and fleeting thought,
But soon I'll land and go to her,
My lover's loving arms.

White on white or white on brown,
The land it rushes by,
And I up here in the high high sky,
As I come to that place of Fate.

In your arms I long to be,
And see your loving arms,
And fears and worries shall fade away,
When you finally hold me, dear.

And until that time as I fly that way,
I'm worrying and freaking out,
But I know all else will fade away,
When our eyes do meet at last.

~March 12, 2015

Longing

Longing, oh longing,
What is longing?
A thousand miles,
Or an inch apart,
Half a decade,
Or a second past,
I long, I long,
The distance grows,
But stays the same,
The time it flutters,
But barely passes,
Each heartbeat,
Each thought,
A body longing,
A soul apart,
My mind it wanders,
Forevermore,
Memories and hopes,
Things lost and found,
And through the years,
Of the second hand,
And miles and miles,
To hold your hand,

My longing flutters,
My longing grows,
And each long second,
Til another rose,
Walk with me,
My hand in yours,
No more longing,
Forevermore,
But each long second,
We are apart,
My longing bursts,
Like a blood red rose,
And so I wonder,
And so I fret,
Of secret glances,
And hungry gasps,
And with my soul,
And heart I call,
Longing, oh longing,
For you my love.

~March 26, 2015

Bethany Davis

Tangible and Clear

Mists condense, now solid form,
Now I have known your touch,
Each little bit, of my fair skin,
Longs for your embrace,
What once was mist, and hope of hope,
I've tasted and I've felt,
And know much more, than passing mist,
Held tight in loving arms,
And mist and shadow, that used to dance,
Now tangible and clear,
No more I long, for what I've never known,
For now I know your touch,
And flights of fancy, now manifest,
Memory is more than thought,
My body longs, for what it's felt,
The mist that then took form,
My solid love, with my own hands,
I held and touched and stroked,
You are not mist, or shadowed hope,
Your darkness I have felt,
And moon and stars, in dark night sky,
Held finally in your arms,
Two wolves we ran, two ravens flew,
Two snakes that twisted round,
Mists condense, and shadows form,
And we are who we are,
No longer thought, of what might be,
The memory of your touch,
Mists condense, and shadows form,
And we are who we are,
And tangible, I've held my love,
And will forevermore.

~March 31, 2015

Bethany Davis

Bethany Davis

Prairie Wind

Down from the heights of mountains white,
Down to the prairie plains,
The prairie winds they call my name,
And one who calls my soul,
My fair night sky, my darkness sweet,
My soul's most precious song,
And there I go for her strong arms,
To hold me evermore,
My gypsy soul is never still,
And always parts and returns,
But in her arms I long to be,
From which I'll never stray,
The glory of the mountain peaks,
And the beauty of the plains,
Ocean waves and crashing tides,
And a city's dancing lights,
Where I roam I'll ever be,
And where I go I go,
And prairie winds they call my name,
And one who calls my soul,
The land it grows and ever moves,
Just like my gypsy soul,
And rushing winds in heights and plains,
And salty gales below,

The wind I be forevermore,
The wind that knows the land,
And where I rest I'll always be,
And where I go I go,
To you I come, my heart, my soul,
With you I long to be,
Upon the peaks or prairies fair,
Or on the crashing waves,
My gypsy soul has wandered wide,
And seen far more than most,
A lonely road with beauty fair,
But lonely all alone,
And to your arms I always go,
My one who calls my soul,
And though we part we always return,
And me into your arms,
So down I go from mountains white,
Down to the prairie plains,
The prairie winds they call my name,
And one who calls my soul,
My fair night sky, my darkness sweet,
My soul's most precious song,
And there I go for her strong arms,
To hold me evermore.

~April 3, 2015

Bethany Davis

Gales

In the cold night I dream of you,
And you are in all my thoughts,
Time moves slow to come to you,
And time it rushes past,
Into your arms I long to come,
Into your sweet embrace,
Soon my love we'll laugh and cry,
In each other's arms.

And though time waits with baited breath,
And my return seems so far away,
I come to you like the prairie wind,
Like a storm from mountain peaks,
Our life is changed but all the same,
For we have always been,
For time apart makes the heart grow fond,
But it hurts like the gales of Hel.

It's cold apart on a winter night,
And more so in the sun,
For far apart we're not meant to be,
We should be in each other's arms,
So as I prepare I long and wait,
Until I come to you,
In the cold night I dream of you,
And you are in all my thoughts.

~April 4, 2015

Bethany Davis

ABOUT THE AUTHOR

Bethany Davis currently resides in a small town in Saskatchewan with her true love. Previously she lived in Colorado and Wyoming, working in technology. She is the proud mother of a fey creature in the form of a cat, adopted mother of a bird in the form of a cat, is a part time vegan and part time meat connoisseur, and a walker of edges. Her life pursuit is to find beauty in all things. Bethany has been writing poetry most of her life, among other pursuits.